STROSE

'13 '14 PROSE

THE COLLEGE OF SAINT ROSE

IIIIIIIIIIIIIIIIIIIIIIIIIIIIIIIIIIIIIIIIIIIIIIIIIIIIIIIIIIIIIIIIIIIIIIIIIIIIIII

an Anthology of First-Year Writing

STROSE
'13 '14 PROSE

PREFACE

Welcome to the seventh edition of Strose Prose. This collection of fourteen essays celebrates the voices and stories of First-Year students enrolled in English 105: Expository Writing, Research Techniques, and Oral Communication at the College of Saint Rose in Albany, New York.

The essays gathered here represent a wide range of subjects and styles, but they are linked by their ability to evoke images, raise questions, conduct research, and transport readers. You'll find essays about coping with the loss of a loved one, the use of iPads in special education classes, and the art of pouring beer. You'll read about current issues in our nation from the politics of fracking to the use of holistic remedies to treat depression. Through their use of description, observation, and investigation, all of the writers in this anthology explore and expand our understanding of the diverse and complex world we live in. Our hope is that this unedited collection of essays will prove useful for first-year students and their instructors as they experiment with the multitude of topics and rhetorical choices available to writers.

Strose Prose would not have been possible without the participation and support of the Saint Rose community. I'd like to thank all the first-year students who submitted their work for consideration and the English 105 instructors who invited their students to submit essays. A big shout-out goes to the English 105 committee for their time and energy: Jennifer Marlow, Kim Middleton, and Dave Rice. Finally, we are excited about our new partnership with The Troy Book Makers—a local publishing company--and the talented team of Jessika Hazelton and Cory Freeman. The book you hold in your hands is truly a collaborative endeavor and we hope you enjoy reading it.

Megan Fulwiler

Coordinator of First-Year Writing

Associate Professor of English

June 2013

TABLE OF CONTENTS

PERSONAL REFLECTION

INQUIRY & RESEARCH

EXPERIMENTAL

DEATH RACE

||||||||||||||||||||||||||||||||||||||||||||||||||||||||||||||||||||||||||||||||||||||||||

Andy Gilchrist

"I ran. I ran until my muscles burned and my veins pumped battery acid. Then I ran some more."   - The Narrator (Fight Club)

0:40:00

I am about to die and I volunteered for it. I have been running for days nonstop and have years to go, yet I cannot rest. I am feeling more pain than humanly possible and it will be beyond unbearable before I am done. My body is literally on fire with nothing but desert before me for hundreds of miles.

None of these things are actually true, but are wild exaggerations of the somewhat endurable conditions I currently find myself under. I am running a half-marathon, 13.1 miles along paved rolling hills with several of my friends. These are the facts: I have been running for about 40 minutes, I have been in extreme pain the entire time, it is over 90 degrees, and I have nearly six more miles to go. I am certain that I could die before I finish.

-17:59:35

It's 4:00 on a Friday. Normally, I would be running inside on the track, unless the gym got too hot and I could barely breathe. On those frequent days, I would go to the weight room and spend 60 to 75 minutes running in place on a treadmill while staring at a TV.

Instead, I am sitting on my ass in front of a computer screen instead of working out. The semester has been done for about a week and I've been soaking up the nothingness of summer vacation. Every afternoon this week, I thought about the big race this Saturday and how I needed to get outside and train for it. But somehow, I just don't care. Relaxing is just too good. Anyway, it's not like it's my first time. I've run a few half-marathons before this one, so I should be fine tomorrow. I shouldn't die.

0:51:01

My legs are made of Jell-O and more muscle cells jump ship with every step I take. My feet slap the pavement, causing my ears to rip open as lighting continues to shoot up my body and almost paralyzes me. My lungs imploded and I coughed them up miles ago, leaving a ball of pure pain in the center of my chest to torment me. The sun continues to walk across the sky and taunt me as it burns and blisters my pathetically pale white skin.

The race officials didn't close off the roads, so traffic still flows freely up and down the rolling hills I suffer on. A car passes by me and though it is four or five feet away, the slight breeze it brushes against my body almost sends me flying backwards like I'm standing behind an airplane turbine. The leaders, guys who actually came prepared, start passing by on the other side of the road, looking as strong as when they started. They could easily run for days on end, yet here I am about to drop dead.

Up ahead, I finally see the turnaround point. At last, halfway.

-0:27:30

I find an excellent parking spot right near the start and there's almost no one at the pre-registered line. I meet up with some of my old high school classmates and teammates who will be running with me; or in front of me, they all joke. We run around the parking lot a little, then onto the track for two laps before stretching. All loosened up, someone asks how much we've all been running since we graduated; everyone says "some, not much." We all talk about how hard it is to find the time and motivation to run since we're all in college now; yet here we are.

A megaphone announces that it is five minutes before the race, so we all head towards the start and push our way to the front of the line; yes, we're those guys. We all tell each other good luck as a starting pistol is raised into the air and all I can think is 'this is going to be a great race.'

1:03:20

It is around mile nine that quitting first creeps into my brain. The continuous rolling hills, the constant up and down, have finally passed and instead I am staring at the longest road ever constructed. I can see heat waves rising up off of it and I expect a giant unicorn or flaming motorcycle, some fantastical mirage, to fly by me. I can no longer feel my legs, feet, or chest and I'm getting dangerously light-headed. I'm massively dehydrated and I'm certain I'm going to throw up within the next few steps. I breathe a sigh of relief when I finally decide to stop.

But I don't. I just keep moving, slowing down to almost nothing, but still maintaining a jog. The machine has taken over; I'm no longer in control of my own body. Years of competitive running and raw willpower don't let me stop. I use an old technique from middle school cross country: look at the next lamppost or stop sign and run to it. Then run to the next one. Keep doing this until you're done.

Despite having been running on empty for the last few miles, I can finally see a turn in the road and the finish is just 200 feet or so beyond that. But even my juvenile techniques are failing me and I'm sure I'm going to stop. I won't finish, I've failed. Just stop. Stop. Stop…

+ 7:26:49

I'm sitting in a cold movie theater watching some new summer blockbuster with a group of friends. The movie starts out with a frantic chase sequence, but evolves into a long drawn out epic with several unimaginable conflicts for the main character. He keeps spiraling further and further down, crying about how much he wants to just shrivel up and die, making us think it will be impossible for me, I mean him, to ever rise again. But he does, somehow surviving every challenge thrown at him and beating the main villain at the end, walking off into the sunset a changed, but stronger, man. As the credits roll, my friends get up and immediately begin dissecting the movie.

"Wow, that was awesome. Great special effects. And the story was really thought out too. When do you think the sequel will be out? I heard they're planning a trilogy. And what about those previews? Not bad, but I've seen them all before. What did you think? Hey, you alright?"

No, I'm not alright. I had the worst experience of my life this morning and for the first time ever, I honestly thought I could die. I did somehow finish that race without stopping, but unlike the man on the screen, I'm not sure that I'm glad I did.

But he's asking me why I'm still sitting through the credits. It's because I can't stand up, my legs won't work. I am broken.

1:32:22 / +0:00:00

I didn't stop. A drop of adrenaline tricked through my scorched veins just before the finish and pushed me a few feet further and past the line. I'm back where I started, standing in the parking lot with other wounded warriors, the scene playing out like an old war movie with soldiers strewn everywhere in various states of pain and suffering. I manage to grab a bottle of water that a child pushes toward me and stumble to the brick wall of an old building nearby.

I scrape down the wall to the soft dirt and try to put my shattered brain back together as I sit there. I truly feel like a different person now that I have finished my Odyssey, having defeated numerous monsters in my mind and returned home to my people and thunderous applause. Though my body has been beaten and shredded like never before, I think that I have become stronger and can face almost anything now. I'm ready to run a 5k tomorrow and a track meet on Tuesday; next weekend I could do it all again and the weekend after that. I'm so strong now that I could–

BLEHHHHH! I shriek as vomit violently and unexpectedly launches from my body. I crumple on the ground as that last bit of strength and humanity I had leaks out of my mouth. I am not strong; I cannot run ever again.

Then, an even more sickening feeling comes over me and I begin to laugh to myself. This has happened before; killing myself during a race and barely surviving, telling myself that I'm ready to do it again. It happened a few weeks ago and a few weeks before that.

And it will happen again a few weeks from today.

MEMORIES FROM A MELANCHOLY TIME

||||||||||||||||||||||||||||||||||||||||||||||||||||||||||||||||||||||||||||||||||||||||

Jacob Mortensen

The photograph is framed in a cheap black novelty frame that had been its home since its birth in the Philadelphia "Adventure Aquarium" which is plastered in bold canary print at the top center, right alongside the white and yellow shark fin logo. The picture has been superimposed upon the image of an open mollusks shell in a sub-aquatic environment sporting various sea life, from a bright yellow seahorse hugging the top left of the shell with its spiny neck, to the frolicking brightly painted clownfish in the lower right. At the bottom of the photograph is the date when it was taken, "August 18, 2009," in white print outlined in an aqua blue. It was taken at the base of a stairwell leading up to an invisible space. The stair case is painted a slate blue and is framed by a glistening silver railing, and at the base of the stairs one can catch a glimpse of white tile flooring. In the background, a glass panel acts as a backdrop covered in the partial outline of some aquatic animal in a frosted light blue. On the right is the partial view of an unknown faceless girl.

The subject of this picture is a woman and her two children. She is tanned and weathered, but in her pale green eyes one can detect both a sense of great pride and a small pang of immense sadness. She is dressed in a plain chocolate colored short sleeved shirt and white pants. Around her neck is a bright silver cross, in her ears a pair of shining sterling feather earrings, and on her head a black hat supporting a pair of sunglasses, shielding her completely hairless head from the sun. She is smiling and her hand is on her youngest son's elbow.

He holds his hands behind his back and stands awkwardly before his mother and elder brother. The boy looks to be around ten when in actuality he is thirteen. He is a bit pudgy, which is evident through his stained grey tee-shirt. On his shirt is a crumpled white name-tag, with the word "VISITOR" in bold letters with his name scrawled out in poorly written printing beneath it. The boy has short blond hair sneaking out from under a blue and white baseball cap; he is smiling, happy and innocent.

Behind the boy his brother, just as awkward looking and also slightly overweight, is dressed in jeans and a brown and white striped polo with designs on each shoulder. Beneath the polo he is wearing a long-sleeved undershirt pushed up to his elbows to hide his biceps. One arm hangs at his side his fingers curled into a fist and the other arm rests on his mother's right shoulder. He is the tallest of the three, has a mass of unkempt brown locks upon his head, and like the other two possesses a grin. One may observe that in his look there is hope and the expectation of disappointment hidden behind his long hair.

The three of them look happy in this frozen moment in time on the 18th of August 2009. They are my family: my mother my brother and I. The photograph was taken on a trip to The Cancer Center of America in Philadelphia where my mother got her treatment. It was four months before she passed away. Like a mug of cocoa on a cold winters day, the sweet memories this picture evokes warm me through, but as the warmth fades I am left with a cold, empty, bitterness, and a nostalgic longing to be back there with her watching the fish swim by happy and carefree.

CULTURES

||||||||||||||||||||||||||||||||||||||||||||||||||||||||||||||||||||||||||||||||

Michaëlle Mugisha

Every day, we hear about how the world is growing into a small global village. People from every corner of the world are meeting or living together, and each one carries his/her culture with him/her. "Culture is the lens through which we perceive and evaluate what is going on around us" (Henslin, 1999:36); we grow up wearing those lenses and learn to act and react according to them. That is how we view the world and we react to it. We are like the fish in the sea that do not know they need water until they are taken out of it; we do not know we need or breathe our culture until we are taken out of it. Culture influences the way people think and how they relate to one another.

We would expect people to be more accepting and more aware of the differences between one another or among nations. Instead, the more we experience the diversity of the world, the more our ethnocentrism grows. We feel that our culture is better than others.

This was my case when I came to the US. I had lived in India for three years and I had traveled to other countries. I always thought of myself as being open minded, and more accepting of differences. When I encountered the American culture, I realized that most people judge because they do not understand the others. Because we know a little, it does not mean we understand the culture. We have to be in that culture to understand people in it, from the other perspective.

The first few months I thought Americans did not have a culture and they were rude. It was such a shock to see that the culture I thought I knew was so disappointing. I thought that being exposed to the popular culture of the US made me an expert on the American culture. I was wrong. I could not appreciate the American culture anymore because I was not in my culture. It was conflicting with who I was and my vision of the world. I was experiencing what the sociologists call "Culture shock".

I did not understand what was going on inside of me. It was hard and confusing. Fortunately, in my first semester among the classes I took, there were two that were valuable. It was intercultural communication and sociology. In these classes, I learned the differences between cultures, the traits of each kind of culture, and who I am. Now I can embrace my identity fully.

The small, insignificant things in my life opened my eyes to a whole new world and I started paying attention to the differences, the values, and traits among cultures. I would like to walk you through the small differences that exist between my culture and the American culture.

For instance, in Burundi, when someone greets you, it means you mean something to him/her. It means he considers you and you expect that person to be your friend in the future. After the greeting, you take time to exchange a few words and there is small conversation. In the US, I noticed that the greetings are just greetings, and they do not mean that the person is interested in making a small chat with you or that you have to be friends or to know each other to greet someone. A small difference of culture like that had never crossed my mind. I expected it to be the same as in Burundi. Here, by the time you say your response to the greeting, the person is already half a mile away from you. It is really impolite in my culture and moreover it hurts because that person did not give you a small portion of his/ her time. I cannot count the number of times I was confused and hurt by people I wanted to greet. I thought these people were being rude to me .Here a greeting is a gesture, but for Burundians it is a symbol of respect and politeness. That is why mostly the greeting includes a handshake or kiss on the cheeks (as we were colonized by Belgium-Wallonia, where French culture is predominant); it was weird for me at first to say hello without shaking one's hand.

Another example is the eye contact. In my culture, we do not maintain eye contact in conversations, especially if it is someone who is older than we. It is considered disrespectful and rude. We tend to be closer to each other along with a small touch on hands and shoulders. On the contrary, it is a sign of respect in the US in conversations. It is very rude and people could be offended if you do not maintain the eye contact. I think this also falls into the personal space differences. Since there is no eye contact for us, we compensate by reducing the personal space. It doesn't mean anything but affection. Here, we have to be careful of the required personal space; otherwise, people think you are a weirdo. In conversation, for outsiders we tend to be close and we have many hand gestures (Illustrators). For the Americans, personal space is wide and few illustrators. This is still the biggest challenge along with eye contact.

Another example is the informal way of addressing elderly persons. Here in the US the level of formality is very low. If you have been introduced to each other, people will call each other by their first names. But the order is formal; Americans in introduction start by the oldest to the youngest.

In Burundi we cannot call someone by his first name unless he/she is your age mate. Each time I try to call my professors by their first names, I feel so uncomfortable and disrespectful. I want to adopt some of the American culture but not at the expense of my culture. I always hope not to look like a weirdo in being so polite and reserved. My second week at Saint Rose, I was dumbfounded by a student answering a question. She was giving an example of her boyfriend and her relationship. For me, that was very informal. How could she talk about something so personal in front of a professor and students? I could not believe it. But that is her culture. I have learned to appreciate every bit of difference I encounter in my life experience. It makes me a better person, more understanding and less quick to judge.

An interesting fact is the individualism façade of the American people. Western culture attempts to encourage the independence of the children by training them to think for themselves, and train them to make their own choices in many areas (Martin and Nakayama).

People in the US dream about the day they become 18 to leave their house and face life on their own. Americans value honesty, openness, and forthrightness (Culture differences). In conversation they are more direct and people take greater pride in individual accomplishments, enjoy more personal freedoms, enjoy more privacy, and live with more spontaneity than people in collectivist cultures, especially for Burundians.

Burundians have a collectivistic culture. Collectivistic cultures encourage the development of group identities by teaching communal sensitivity and cooperation, and advising the child on important matters (Martin and Nakayama). We like being around family and we always want to ask someone of our family to help face life or to make it. We feel that our families are there to give us a hand (jobs, personal advice, conflicts). We put our families first (opinions, decisions). We do not have a direct speech. We "beat around the bush" in a conversation. We avoid confrontation and confrontational issues. We also work on cultivating long-term relationships without expecting instant closeness (Cultural differences); we present ourselves modestly and pay attention to people's positions in any hierarchies. An American might be bored by the level of title that a subordinate gives to a high officer (My director, my dear honorable minister, etc.). Burundians also use titles or status instead of name. For examples, my friends use "Papa Michaëlle" to call my father instead of using his name. If it is the first time you would think that they are hypocrites or foolish people but that is who we are and how we view the world. All those titles, respect and indirectness make our society work for our own good.

So when we travel to some other places, we carry that heavy luggage: our culture, our lens of viewing the world. We do not leave them in America or in Burundi; but it is part of who we are and what we have to offer to anyone who comes to our way. That's part of the contribution we give to the world. It comes with the trademarks and the fingerprints of our different cultures, of our different personalities. We have to treasure our culture because the beauty of this world lies in its diversity

Works Cited

"Culture and Society" Socio blog. Web. 20 Mar.2013
< http://socioanthero.blogspot.com/p/culture-and-society.html >

"Cultural Differences." Cultural Differences. Web. 20 Mar. 2013
<http://homepages.rpi.edu/~verwyc/oh5.htm>Martin,

Judith; and Thomas Nakayama "Experiencing Intercultural Communication: An Introduction, 4th Edition" Print. October 2012.

ANTHROPOMORPHISM

||||||||||||||||||||||||||||||||||||||||||||||||||||||||||||||||||||||||||||||

Erin O'Sullivan

Since I was a toddler I have always been passionate about animals, and over the years, I have been my neighborhood's designated pet sitter or dog walker. From the time I was in fourth grade I have always had a pet, whether it was a hermit crab, chameleon, frog, or bearded dragon. Unusual pets are a norm in my house because my father has terrible allergies to all things furry and fluffy. One of my neighbors, an owner of several cats for which I provided care, accused me of practicing anthropomorphism, not only due to my comments regarding his cats, but especially with my descriptions of behaviors and interactions associated with my own non-mammalian pets. Perhaps my neighbor was correct about my anthropomorphic ways. For I believe I have witnessed my crustaceans, amphibians, and reptilian pets demonstrate the human emotions of curiosity, contentment, compassion, and commitment, and display unexpected bonding that is reminiscent of human love and, when love is lost, grief.

Since hermit crabs are social creatures, many crabs lived in the sand-filled glass terrarium in the corner of my room, each possessing carefully selected and adorable names such as Scampi, Scooter, Pincher, Nemo, Dory, Spot, and Buttons, to name a few. Dory and Nemo were purchased simultaneously from a pet store where they had shared the same home, and thus, when brought to my terrarium, were inseparable. Dory and Nemo lived healthily for several months, until Dory became ill and died. Upon Dory's death, Nemo became distraught, abandoned his shell, ran aimlessly around the enclosure, and despite my efforts to have him reenter any shell, he perished. Having observed Dory and Nemo's special relationship, it was obvious that Nemo's drastic reaction was caused by grief.

African Clawed aquatic frogs are also social creatures, developing complex relationships and exhibiting great curiosity. When my mother read me bedtime stories or when music was playing, the frogs would float to the water's surface to listen. Once, when Shamrock, the large female frog, escaped from the aquarium, her smaller male companion, Emerald, became surprisingly frantic, swimming rapidly in the water while croaking more loudly than ever before. Upon Shamrock's capture and return, Emerald ceased his croaking and clung tightly to her. Compassion is another trait the frogs seem to possess, as demonstrated by the tireless efforts of Rainbow, who kept his ill frog friend afloat as he took his last breaths.

The three Chameleons, with which I have been privileged to share my home, were filled with personality and showed affection towards my family. Olive, a beautiful, young, velvety green Veiled Chameleon, and Elroy, a brightly colored red, green-and-turquoise striped Panther Chameleon, both indicated a strong desire to leave their habitats whenever a family member was in sight, as they would run to the screened door of their enclosure and press their mitten hands against the door. Otto, my three-horned Jackson Chameleon with droopy-drawer legs, never protested and always nestled tightly when I placed him into my silky psychedelic Groovy-Girl doll bed and covered him with a velvet blanket, as I sat at the dinning room table and did my homework.

I never imagined I could learn so much about the traits that we think make us human as I have by caring for and observing multiple species. Under different circumstances, I never would have expected such unusual pets, which are normally considered non-interactive, to help me understand the exciting ways of diverse life forms, and to help me realize how all creatures are similarly interconnected. Just as I have learned through my pets, everyone, including animals, is unique with individual personality traits waiting to emerge.

A "FISH STORY"

||||||||||||||||||||||||||||||||||||||||||||||||||||||||||||||||||||||||||||

Joseph Russell

The water reflected the beautiful surrounding mountains and the clear blue sky like a mirror that morning. Auger Island stood still in the distance, it was early, 5 am, and not a single wave rippled across the water. My father and I took the canoe from the bed of our faithful Chevy, set it on the dock and embraced the view. My sister, Karli, hopped out of the truck, camera in hand, sipping her freshly brewed hot chocolate. Dad went to park the truck and Karli and I stood droopy eyed next to the water, anxiously awaiting his return.

It was early summer and we were on our favorite vacation of the year, our annual trip to Limekiln Lake. We traveled two and a half hours for a week of camping, boating, hiking, fires, and all around fun. This was our time together as a family; it was something we all enjoyed and something we had done for years. Everybody had their favorite activity, but for me it was to hit the lake, with a fishing pole and my father. Since I was young, he and I had always been fishing buddies. We spent weekend after weekend heading to different lakes, ponds and streams. We did this in all seasons, trying to land a big one, but above all else, we enjoyed each other's company. I was always taught that fishing was a get-away; a time where we could leave our hectic lives, forget the troubles of the week, and step

17

back from the responsibilities we had. This was our escape, and we were happy to be there.

I sipped my coffee and checked over the boat to make sure we had all our gear. As usual, it was packed. Tackle boxes, fishing poles, life vests, and paddles covered the floor. Dad returned, smiling as always, and asked, "We ready?" Karli and I smiled and nodded. "1, 2, 3," he counted, and we picked up our loaded canoe and set it in the water, causing the first ripple of the day. Karli stepped in while dad and I held the boat steady. She sat down, put on her life vest, and settled in. Dad and I then got in and we were off. The lake was quiet; the only audible sound was that of the birds chirping and our paddles entering the water.

"Daddy, can you worm me?" Karli broke the silence. I chuckled and he obliged. Even after 14 years of fishing, she still wasn't comfortable touching a dirty slimy worm and putting it on her hook. We drifted down shore and we began fishing. CLICK ZZZZ, our poles spoke as we casted out and retrieved. Karli started us off, catching small sunfish and perch, becoming more and more excited with each fish. Although she usually only caught smaller fish, she was consistent and she enjoyed it. She reeled them in and swung them to my father, she wasn't ready to take her own fish off the hook either.

"What a beautiful morning," Dad commented.

"Sure is," I replied.

"What are you usi --"

"Daddy, I got another!!" he was interrupted and Karli reeled in a sunny. She was bringing them in non-stop, keeping my father busy with re-worming, and unhooking. I always felt bad for my father, most of his time fishing was spent doing everything but that. He baited Karli's hook, paddled us around, untangled our knots, and would even give up his own pole if we needed it. It always seemed that not a minute could pass where Karli or I didn't have an issue that required his attention. But Dad was there for us, so he didn't mind.

I casted into shore, out to the deep, and caught nothing but some weeds and sticks. I decided to put on my stand by. What my father and I affectionately refer to as "the clown." This was a red, white, yellow Rapala (fishing lure brand) that mimicked the motion of a minnow swimming in the water. We had always had great luck with this color scheme, and I figured it was about time I switched to it.

I attached the lure to my swivel and began casting. I was confident in my lure, and figured it was only a matter of time before something hit. Dad paddled occasionally to keep us slowly coasting down the lake. We entered a picture perfect cove that looked as if it was out of a fishing magazine. Stumps and logs poked out of the water, and tall pines stood like towers on the shore, providing plenty of cover from the increasingly higher sun. Mist rose off the water as we slowly glided in. I mentioned to my father how perfect this spot seemed. We casted left and right, reeling and working our lures, hoping for anything. Finally, a hit, my pole flexed and bent nearly in half, this was a monster. I hollered, "I got one!" My sister and father reeled in and watched. The front end of the canoe shifted towards the fish, and my father aided and rapidly paddled towards the end of my line, coaching me through the fight, "Don't force it! Let 'em tire out! Don't break the line!"

After what seemed like an eternity, I was finally able to real the giant in. It surfaced next to the canoe and the monsters head peaked out of the water, his eyes glistening in the sunlight. Battle scars covered his massive drab green body. The murky stench of the lake bed filled the air as he hovered at the surface. It was a northern pike, and a monster at that. The fish of my dreams floated motionless next to the canoe. I screamed, "GET THE NET!" This fish was bigger than any I had ever seen. My dad replied sorrowfully, "There is no net." And with a flick of his massive tail, he snapped the line, and off he went, with my precious clown lure hanging from his mouth. I had lost it. My stomach turned and my face fell into my hands. I felt like I would be sick. We sat silent, disgusted at our loss. CLICK ZZZ, the silence was broken as Karli giggled and casted out. Dad tried to console me but there was no use, I was devastated. I had lost the fish of a life time, thanks to some cheap fishing line, and the lack of a net.

For a long time, I was bitter about that day, hearing the jokes from friends and family about a "fish story" only lead to feelings of malice. It is hard not to relive that moment every time I pick up my pole, or get in the canoe. Overtime however, thoughts of 'what could have been' faded. In all honesty, at times the thought of that morning still eats at me, but I've learned to embrace it. When it is mentioned I laugh and brush it off. I now realize I was never there for the fish; I was there for my Dad, and the memory we would always share, of the monster we lost on 4th Lake.

I AM WHO I AM

|||||||||||||||||||||||||||||||||||||||||||||||||||||||||||||||||||||||||||

Stephen Schillat

"Alright, everyone get into groups of four for the next activity. You can pick your own partners." My heart sinks a bit in my chest at my teacher's last sentence. I nervously glance around at my other classmates, who've already found their group members. Yet I remain, singled out. "Ah- Stephen, just pick one of the groups and make a group of five." I survey the room again, hearing faint whispers of "Ugh, not Stephen…" mixed with "Ew, he's fuckin' gay." Eventually, I join the least objectionable group, ignoring their painfully obvious exasperated sighs. It's nothing new to me. I've been shunned for being bisexual since before I even knew what "gay" meant.

The 5th grade can be a harsh time for someone who is belittled for being himself, and I found that out firsthand. Of course, nobody could have actually known about my sexuality back then. Not even I had known. No, I was called "gay" not because of my "deviant lifestyle" as some right-wing politicians might label it, but because I was the "weird" kid. For many, "gay" is just another word used to describe something you don't like. I just happened to be that unfortunate "something." But while my peers' ridicule may have been misspoken, it was actually not far from the truth.

In the years after elementary school, I learned to put the past behind me. Middle school brought with it new people, a fresh start. And as long as I steered clear of any unwelcome encounters with old classmates, the rumors that had once terrorized me dwindled down to mere unpleasant memories. But the hurtful words I endured could never truly be forgotten. To this day, I still shudder when I think about it. When reminded of my 5th grade experience, I instinctively take the emotional defensive and reject the accusations of my verbal attackers. I knew that I was wrongfully abused with icy words like "gay" and "fag," words that sting more than salt poured into an open wound. It was the emotional scars left by those icy words that made me question my sexuality in high school. Looking back, it's no wonder why I became aware of my sexuality in high school and not in the years before. Puberty in full bloom, testosterone galore, some things perking up while others drop down; mother nature is a pro boxer who bides her time, waiting for the opportune moment to strike you right where the sun doesn't shine, like a sucker punch of sexuality. Try as you might to avoid each blow, she'll always have a right hook prepared to knock you down for the count. Resistance is futile.

Before I fully sorted out my sexuality, I became very frustrated. Every time I felt lust towards another male, I was reminded of the horrible treatment I received from my peers in 5th grade. This made accepting myself even more difficult. The way I saw it at the time was that if I accepted my attraction to men, I would be confirming every hurtful word I'd been called. The thought of lowering myself to match the same disgusting terms that were used to antagonize me truly sickened me, but what sickened me even more was the sense of being controlled by people I despised. No…the MEMORY of them. There is no greater shame than becoming a slave to words forgotten by those who spoke them. The words of others can only influence you as much as you allow them to. Just because I was labeled a "gay fag" didn't mean that I had to relinquish my attraction for women any more than I would if I was called "dish soap" or "tree bark." I knew that. And it didn't mean that I had to deny my attraction towards men either. It's the combination of both attractions that have shaped me into who I am, and accepting that has made me a stronger person. I refuse to let words of ignorance and bigotry define who I am. I define who I am. These feelings did not come without their fair share of trepidation though.

While accepting my sexuality was a huge step forward for me, other people are not often as open-minded or understanding. I knew that there were other members of the LGBT community among the students in my high school, but I knew none of them. It's not like they suddenly broke into song and dance, dressed head to toe in peacock feathers as they waved rainbow flags around (though I'll admit that it would've been helpful if they did). For a while, I felt alienated, as if I was the only bisexual around, until I met Fantasia.

Fantasia was an openly bisexual girl that I'd met on the last day of my sophomore year of high school. We got along really well, and quickly became friends. We even ended up going to a carnival the next day, and when it got late, we sat together on the edge of the sidewalk under the Ferris wheel while we waited for our rides to come pick us up. While we waited, three guys passed over us in the Ferris wheel. One of them saw us and shouted, "Hey, you're gay!" I chose to ignore it thinking, "Whatever, it's not like I haven't heard this before." Fantasia, however, reacted quite differently. She quickly spotted the jerk and shouted back at him, though him and his friends were safely in the air above us where Fantasia's words only made them laugh. When she wasn't shouting threats, Fantasia was gritting her teeth in fury. I sighed passively, assuming that it was over when the teasing stopped being heard from above, but to Fantasia, this was far from settled. She took off towards the Ferris wheel's exit gate and waited there in scornful silence, well, for about three seconds until she saw the group who thoughtlessly heckled our nice time. I followed her there and stared in awe as she confronted the guy who shouted at us and mercilessly berated him for his words. "WHO DO YOU THINK YOU ARE!? YOU THINK THAT WAS FUNNY?" Clearly, neither he nor his friends were expecting this as they could think of no response other than quiet, nervous laughter. When he tried to walk away, Fantasia followed, her yelling growing in volume. A few passersby watched nervously as the yelling ensued. At that moment, I took it upon myself to hold Fantasia by the arm, allowing the three now-silenced teens to walk away. If I hadn't stopped her, I'm sure she would've done a lot more than just yell, but once she calmed down, we both laughed about it until our rides came. Unfortunately, she moved to Pennsylvania within the next few days and we lost touch, so the friendship was short lived. The impact she had on my life however, lasts to this day.

In the short time that I knew her, Fantasia was one of the most influential people I'd ever met. She wasn't just any bisexual; she was the first one I'd met that wasn't afraid to be true to herself, and be loud and proud about it. She possessed unshakeable courage and wouldn't stand for anyone who had the nerve to speak poorly of the LGBT community. For me, meeting Fantasia was the first major step I took in coming to realize that being bisexual isn't something to be ashamed of; it's something to be proud of.

Discovering and accepting my sexuality has given me so much depth in my life. It's made me more confident, more open-minded, more understanding, and I've never been happier. It does have its obvious drawbacks, though. It's made me a target for sexuality discrimination, forcing me to be more cautious around new people. I cannot safely enjoy the sandy beaches of Jamaica, lest I risk subjecting myself to violent acts of homophobia. I am now an "enemy" in the eyes of various religious institutions. But despite the obstacles I face, I'm not ashamed of my sexuality. It's a consistent, inherent quality from which I can draw inspiration and the courage to be who I am. It's made me stronger than I'd ever be otherwise, and I'm proud to be part of something as colorful, diverse, and resilient as the LGBT community. Being a bisexual gives me a sense of liberation and belonging. Nothing else has ever hit so close to home, to the very core of who I am.

MOMMA'S GONNA BUY YOU A MOCKINGBIRD

||||||||||||||||||||||||||||||||||||||||||||||||||||||||||||||||||||||||||||||||||||||||||||||

Erica Schipani

My words are shaky and my body's trembling. I was always scared to tell her anything bad. "I can't talk to you anymore, it's too much stress on me" are the words that shot through the phone to her numb ear. Of course she didn't understand. She never understood. Selfish. Her reply sent guilt through my veins but I stood my ground. It was my senior year in high school. This was an important year. I was done with the bullshit. She asked how long I needed. I didn't know.

1999

I can't remember the month or day. All I remember was jumping up and down on my living room couch with my brother. Screams and cries down the hall lead to my parents' bedroom. My brother was told to keep me occupied every time this happened. Why were they screaming? Why did my Dad look so sad all the

25

time? I never understood it. I never understood why he carried me from my bed in the middle of the night into the car to look for her. Why is she doing this? I wish I had the answers at that time, but I never could figure her out. I saw her cooking in the kitchen and cleaning the living room. I felt her hugs, smelled her auburn hair. She dressed me and told me she loved me. But I just couldn't connect beyond the surface. She was just there, no emotion.

January 1999

We're in Brooklyn. It is cold and all I hear is the obnoxious honking from cars and my mother closing the door behind me. It's a two-family apartment. She holds my hand and leads me to the basement apartment down by the garage. It's all blurry to me. A man opens the door and stands at average height, no more than twenty seven years old. We walk in: a full size bed, a kitchen fit for once person, and a bathroom you'd find on a boat. That's what I stared at for five minutes. I didn't know him. And that's where he tells me to look, "Just look this way for a minute." My mother didn't say anything.

2003

I'm sitting on the black leather couch and this fat short woman with square-shaped glasses is looking at me. I remember what I was wearing that day: my yellow camisole with yellow roses on it with my yellow sweater over it. I loved that outfit. My dad and brother come in the room and sit down. She asks me if I know why I'm there, I reply with a no. "We're all here to tell you that your mother has been abusing drugs." Numb. I'm eight years old, who hears that at eight years old? The only words I could find from the limited amount in my head were,

"My mom? How could my mom be on drugs?" And the woman in the computer chair proceeded to say,

"She has been since she was young and you're parents are getting divorced and this is the reason why."

She walks in the room. I don't know what to do. I was young and naive, so naturally I tell her it's okay and that I still love her. My brother was next. He was so angry. Why was he so angry? She's our mom. She'll get better. My brother expressed his anger towards her. I was watching him in awe. Was I supposed to feel this way too? We both left the session on opposite ends.

2007

We're sitting in our favorite sushi restaurant and it's happening again. She's looking at me as I'm speaking but her eyes are slowly closing. Like wings, they shutter up and down. But with the efforts to stay awake and look normal, her eyeballs vibrate at the strain of it. Her head slowly droops, but she quickly catches this. It droops again: down, down, drop. Filled with embarrassment, I kick her shin. "Ow, Erica!" she says. "You were falling asleep again, Mom." That's what I told myself it was, she was just really tired. After our alert three minute conversation, she goes to the bathroom. Oh no, why? I hate when she goes to the bathroom. Five minutes goes by and I know I'll be waiting longer. I feel the whole room staring at me and I become hot and sweaty. Everyone's probably wondering why she's taking so long. Fuck, they know. I had no control, the room was spinning and I was staring at my California Roll, the only thing I could focus on. She finally comes out and my stomach is done turning. No one's staring at me anymore.

We're ready to leave and the short Asian man places the check on the table with a worried expression. I hated this part whenever we went out to eat. Half the time she didn't have enough money and we'd have to call my dad to come by and pay the rest. She opens her wallet and my heart's thumping out of my flat chest. She's bustling around and all I see is a twenty dollar bill and some food benefit cards. She finds enough and I can let go of my breath.

October 2009 7:00 PM

I'm in Manalapan, New Jersey, my mother's new home. For her this was a new start. She had a job, clean friends and rent paid. We're taking a drive to her friend TJ's she tells me. As we pull up to the house, all I see is filth: the windows look as if someone's tried to break in and the front door's paint is scratched. Her friend pulls up in the driveway and they stumble out of the car. A middle-aged man stomps his Timberland boot down on the driveway with a disgruntled look. And TJ: she's so thin, maybe about 50 years old, with a drooping mouth and eyes. Her words slur and my mom even looks embarrassed. She says, "I'll call you later" and we left. That night we ordered food and watched movies. I loved spending this time with her, it's what I had missed for most of my life. Little did I know this was toxic. That night, I crawl into my mother's bed, turn on my side and fall asleep.

She's in the damn bathroom again. It's midnight and I'm trying to sleep. I really can't sleep this time because my grandma's away and I never feel safe when I'm alone with her. She's made too many bad deals with people: people that would threaten her. They know where she lives and they know who I am.

It's 3 AM and I hear the television. She's up. I turn over and she's snacking on pretzel sticks and sipping Seltzer. She always did this. The drugs disturbed her sleeping patterns and I had to take the brunt of every side effect. She only stays up for ten minutes. I grab the remote and turn it off. When she wakes up from her cat nap, she whines, "What are you doing? I was watching that," I ignore her knowing the same pattern is about to occur. She always falls back asleep.

June 2011

I'm sitting in my dad's office working on my homework when I hear my brother screaming and cursing in the kitchen. "You're really a piece of shit, I can't fucking believe you," travels down the hallway. I turn away from my work and my heart starts racing. I wait until he's off the phone and ask what's going on. "Mom got arrested," he said while he slammed the phone on the charger.

What the fuck? My heart goes faster and I'm shaky. I want to cry but pound my fist in the wall at the same time. How? How'd she let it get this bad?

"What happened?" I ask my dad.

"Your mom was at TJ's house, where they sell. And an undercover cop came to buy drugs and busted her."

Disgust is all I could feel throughout my body. She fucking took me there. She made me believe this was just a friend of hers. I went inside that house. I trusted my mother. What else is a daughter supposed to do? If I was there, I could've got arrested too. What the hell was she thinking? She never thought, though. All she thought about was her next high, regardless if I was with her. She couldn't separate her two worlds, so she brought me into it.

August 2011

I open the door and my eyes go to the marks on her chest. Between her legs and her arms, I guess she had no veins left. Her eyes look like mini M&Ms. The image of me telling her to leave and slamming the door crossed my mind. But the wanting of my mother took over. She's crying. What now?

"I just can't win," she says.

"What happened, Mom?"

"I rear-ended someone on the highway." Another accident. I lost count after the first five.

And that's what the rest of her visit was based on. She took my cellphone to make calls to her "friends" in New Jersey to fix her car. She realizes I'm pissed and asks me what's wrong. I finally just say it, "You're high."

"No I'm not Erica, I'm just exhausted." Lies. Why can't she just tell me the truth already?

She goes through the fridge and takes out ham, cheese, and honey Dijon mustard. Her hands are slow and I just watch her make a simple task tedious and drawn out. It's as if she forgot how to use her motor skils. Her head's drooping again as she puts the slice of ham on the bread. Her hand stays there for a moment. All I want to do is push her out of the way and make it for her. But she finally gets it and sits down. She can't do one thing at a time, her brain can't handle calmness, she lives for the chaos. She grabs a piece of paper and a pen as she asks, "Wherrre's ya broth...er?"

"He's out, he knew you were coming today."

"Just leave this note in his room for me."

It took her half an hour to write five sentences. I sat there and watched this. I wanted her to leave so bad. I just wanted the sensation of having to throw up to go away. She starts off on a good start, just writing away, then it happens again. Her swollen hand goes limb and her eyes fall.

I tell her I'm going out. I just couldn't sit there anymore. I can't believe she came here this high. But then again, what else would I expect? Before she leaves, she gives me a big hug. I embrace this. I smell cigarettes on her hair and the drugs on her clothes. But the sweet scent of Cherry Blossom always remained in the mix. She is so skinny, it's so easy to hold her tight. I wish she didn't feel this frail and I wish she wouldn't get into the car again. She was always so lucky. She always made it out alive. So, I take in this fragile moment and tell her I love her. And every time I smell Cherry Blossom, I close my eyes and see my mother.

BABY, DO YOU HEAR THAT?

||||||||||||||||||||||||||||||||||||||||||||||||||||||||||||||||||||||||||||||||||||||||

Kristin Carr

You're Having a Baby!

"It's positive!" You hold in your hand the truth, a white stick with a plus sign displayed on one end. You are going to bring a new life into this world and you have never been so happy in your entire life. Then it sinks in, the anxiety, nervousness and confusion. You may start to read books or magazines and go to classes on parenting, but who knows if everything you think you know is true. Through your studies you come to a long-debated topic about classical music and how it can make babies smarter and their brains grow bigger. Now you want to know more…

The thought of playing music for your unborn child may seem ridiculous at first, but research has been done and the results may cause you rethink the idea. Many studies have been done regarding the use of classical music and the impact it may or may not have on a fetus and infants. So the question is, does music truly impact their brains or is it just another myth to be ridiculed?

The Brain and its Development

It is important for you to first understand the basics of fetal and infant brain development. As a fetus your brain begins to develop just 16 days after conception. The neural plate that has already formed will begin to get longer and fold over to fuse shut after 22 days. The neural plate will be completely shut by the 27th day. At this time the newly formed tube will start to develop into the brain and spinal cord. After five weeks from conception the synapses begin to form in the spinal cord. Synapses are the areas between neurons that the electrical signals are transmitted through to get from one neuron to the next. Neurons are the part of the brain that carry the signals around the brain. The electrical signals will travel through the synapse in chemical packets and received by the receptors of the next neuron. The last part of the brain to form is the cerebral cortex. The cerebral cortex is the part of the brain responsible for voluntary actions, thinking, remembering and feeling.

After six weeks from conception neural connections will allow the fetus to make some movements. After nine weeks the fetus can hiccup and react to certain loud sounds with movements. As time progresses parts of the fetus begin to have the ability to move. By the end of the first trimester an increased amount of fetal movement is happening though the mother usually does not notice. By the end of the second trimester the fetus can perform breathing, sucking and swallowing movements which will be some of the most essential activities the baby needs. Along with these movements developing by the end of the second trimester, the fetus will also develop its hearing. Near the end of the pregnancy the baby has the ability to see. During the last trimester the fetus is capable of simple forms of learning and habituation to a repeated auditory stimulus (Zero to Three). For example, if a fetus repeatedly hears a simple noise from the mother's environment, it will adapt to it and will not be frightened.

The brain develops based on two things: genes and the environment. Genes develop the physical structure of the brain while the environment allows the brain to make connections. The experiences you have impact the structure and connections throughout the brain. This is because the brain is activity-dependent. Activity-dependent means that for our brains to develop and learn it must experience life. Neural circuits make connections between our experiences and what our surroundings mean. The neural circuits in our brains are not fixed structures. This means that during certain activities some neural circuits will be active while others are inactive. The neural circuits that are very active begin to strengthen because they are used more consistently. The inactive neural circuits, on the other hand, weaken and eventually just fall away.

The process of getting rid of the inactive, weakening neural circuits while maintaining the active, strong neural circuits is called pruning. Pruning continues to occur throughout a person's whole life, but it has been found that pruning is most active during early childhood. Because pruning is most active in early childhood it is correct to say that it is the most critical time for brain development. Children are constantly making connections in their brain based on their environment because everything is new to them.

As a newborn our brains are only one quarter of our adult brains. By the age of three our brains are 80% of our adult brains and 90% by the age of five (Zero to Three). Our brains grow drastically at these early ages because changes are constantly being made to the individual neurons.

Research about the Impacts of Music

In order for music to impact fetal brain development researches had to know if in fact a fetus is able to hear. Studies have been done to determine if the fetus does in fact hear or not. One experiment was done by J. P. Lecanuet, C. Graniere-Deferre and A.-Y. Jacquet from the University of Paris with A. J. DeCasper from the University of North Carolina at Greensboro. They tested the cardiac responses that a 36-39 week old fetus has to two low pitch piano notes, D4 and C5, and if they can recognize the difference. Seventy percent of the fetus tested responded to the first note with a deceleration in heart rate. The fetus was then played the other note. Ninety percent of the fetus that responded to the first note had another heart rate deceleration to this note (Lecanuet). These results show that fetus can, not only hear, but also distinguish the differences in tones as well as respond to them. Fetus do not understand what it is they hear, unfortunately, but their brains are processing that it's occurring.

"Firstart" is a program created by Manuel Alonso and Rosa Plaza. In this program graduated violin sounds or parental voices are played for the fetus to hear through a small tape player speaker worn on a belt on the mother's waist (Chamberlain). The expecting mothers had played a total of 70 hours of classical music to their baby from 28 weeks after conception to birth. Psychologists from the University of Valencia found a way to measure the possible results of the program. They decided to take the first measurement when the infants were six months old. Using the chart that psychologists had created mothers recorded what the observed about the behavior of their babies. The stimulated babies displayed more advanced results in language development, gross and fine motor skills, and some cognitive behavior. Between six and twelve months there was a narrowing gap between the development of the stimulated and non-stimulated babies (Chamberlain). It was concluded that the largest difference in a behavior was the understanding of language. This is believed to be true because the baby's auditory sensory was stimulated much more for those participating in the program compared to those that were not.

In 1986, Rene Van de Carr of Hayward, California, experimented with prenatal stimulation. In his study he had 50 fetuses completely participating in his program, 50 fetuses partially participating in his program, and 50 fetuses that would not participate in his program at all. His program consisted of playing classical music and voices for the unborn baby. In his results he found that the fully stimulated fetus did have different behaviors and further brain development. There was a difference in speech, physical growth, parent-infant bonding and success in breast feeding (Chamberlain). He then went on to a write a book that would help expecting mothers understand what they can do to stimulate the fetal brain. In the book, While You are Expecting: Create Your Own Prenatal Classroom, he writes, "There is a critical time in an infants developments beginning at about five months into pregnancy. Interaction between the baby and its environment stimulate brain growth both before and after birth" (Van de Carr 14). He also claims that parents should not over-stimulate the fetus because eventually it will tune out the music due to habituation, which they acquire fairly early into pregnancy.

We also know that a baby can recognize songs they have heard as a fetus. Michael P. Lynch, an associate professor of audiology and speech sciences at Purdue University in West Lafayette, Indiana, said, "Until the past decade, no one knew if infants remembered music in any way. We now know that newborns can even recall music they've heard before birth," (Heller). It has been found that the music being played during the third trimester is the music the baby remembers. When the music heard while in the womb is played to the infant, the baby tends to feel comforted because they recognize the song. Carol Krumhansl, Ph.D., is a psychology professor at Cornell University. She studied infants understanding of certain pitches. She noted that if a three-month-old infant were to be sung a note at a certain pitch, the child would have the ability to repeat the same note almost perfectly. She also preformed a study with four and a half to six month old infants and their responses to the playing of Mozart. In this study she would play sections of Mozart minuets and stop the music at the end of the section or in the middle of the section. She found that most infants would pay more attention when the music stopped at the end correct ending. Krumhansl said, "A musical passage is similar to a sentence, because it generally ends with a drop in pitch and a longer tone. We think infants use the same part of their brains to organize both music and language into understandable segments," (Heller). This means that a baby's brain is stimulated and aware when listening to music than most would infer. They make connections to language as they listen to music and relate the pitches and tones to one another. They have the ability to pick up on what the tones of voices imply, meaning they can interpret when a person is done talking or if they will continue to talk.

What is the Truth?

We know that music will not not make a baby's IQ score higher, nor will the size of their brain increase; we do know, however, that by playing music to a fetus or infant will cause responses in the brain. These responses in the brain imply that neural circuits are being used and activated. The activity of the neural circuits causes brain development in fetus and infants. The development that is occurring should not be mistaken as the child becoming smarter. Just because the fetus' brain is developing does not mean the child is smarter than he/she would have been. Yes, the activity in the brain is at a higher level than if music were not used, but that doesn't have to do with being any smarter. The idea that the brain increases in size with the playing of classical music is also a myth. After all the studies and research done, no results concluded that the brain was larger than normal.

Exposing your infant to music can enhance their ability to process information and stimulate language development. The music encourages the baby to focus on his/her listening skills as they hear the repeating sounds.

Playing certain types of music can also impact the emotions of the baby. If the infant is listening to calm, classical music they tend to fall asleep and feel very relaxed. If the infant is listening to upbeat music they will be more active and awake. Listening to these types of music does bring joy to babies and will arise certain emotions. Classical music proves to have the most impact on the brain due to the complex structure. Fetus and babies are aware of the structure and that's what attracts them to it. The playing of classical music has also been found to have a short-term affect on spatial skills.

Mothers Know Best

After being informed about the truths of brain development and the impacts of classical music, it is up to you to decide where to go from here. Your child may not be getting smarter through listening to classical music, but the music will stimulate the brain and reinforce development. If you chose not to play classical music to your baby, the brain will still develop normally; music will just speed up the process and develop some music-oriented parts of the brain that normally wouldn't develop at that age. Here are some things that you can do that will promote a healthy start to their brain development: You can play music for your baby, after birth and/or before birth. You don't necessarily need to play classical music, though it is the most affective due to the more complex structure that your baby has the ability to remember. Classical music generally consists of the musical workings of Bach, Mozart or Beethoven. The structure of the music is best if it is 60 beats per minute because that is similar to the heart rate of the mother (Sorgen). Bonnie Ward Simon, a music educator, author and president of Magic Music Maestro says, "Parents have to make sure that visuals don't overtake them. The visual sense does take over very quickly. There's too much look and not listen today. If you have a child listening early on, they develop that sense and a sense of imagination"(Benitez). This explains how music will stimulate the mind and help child's imagination grow and develop. You must also be cautious about the volume that the music is being played, especially to the fetus. You should not put headphones on the belly to play music. The amniotic fluid in the womb acts as an amplifier to the fetus and the noises surrounding them. Gary Brody, president of Lovely Baby Music (classical music produced specifically for the developing brain) puts it into perspective, "Imagine you are in a metal garbage can and someone starts banging on the side"(Brody). This is the type of environment that the fetus lives in and explains how volume must be taken into consideration or the baby's hearing could be harmed.

You can also sing to your baby. If you are the mother of the baby it will comfort them to hear your voice because they have the ability to remember it from being in the womb. If you are the father or any other caregiver hearing your voice will give the baby the ability to get to know your voice so that you are no longer a stranger. Singing to your child will also help them learn language, especially as they start to get older. It is easier for the infants to learn words and basic lyrics that will stick with them for the rest of their lives.

If you want your child to learn to play a musical instrument you should start them on lessons earlier than you would intend (Bales). Due to the fact that your child's mind is so fresh and constantly making new connections meaning that learning music is so natural at this time. The children will not learn much, but they will have the ability to learn the basics, which will lead to success with music in the future. You should also know that playing classical music while pregnant can help not only you baby, but also you if you are the mother. Classical music calms people down and will reduce your stress level resulting in a healthier baby (Benitez). If a mother experiences too much stress or anger while they are pregnant it can have negative implications on the child, so by calming yourself down you can help the baby's development as well. Now you know the myths and truths about music's impact on brain development. The brain does not become physically larger, and your child will not magically be smarter than the rest of the kids in class, but music will stimulate the brain and assist in its development. The influences of music start when your child is just a fetus and continues throughout life. So why not expose your baby to classical music if it will lead to faster brain development and a love for a now underrated genre? The decision to try will only lead you and your child to a healthy and positive start to your lives together. Go ahead and do it.

Works Cited

Bales, Diane. "Building Baby's Brain: The Role of Music." *Better Brains for babies*. The University of Georgia/College of Family and Consumer Sciences, Sep. 1998. Web. 7 Dec. 2012. <http://www.fcs.uga.edu/ext/pubs/chfd/FACS01-7.pdf>.

Benitez, Tina. "Experts Discuss Whether Mozart Really Does Make Babies Smarter." *Fox News*. Fox News Network, 26 Sep. 2007. Web. 12 Dec. 2012. <http://www.foxnews.com/story/0,2933,297994,00.html>.

Brink, Donna. "Music and Baby's Brain." *Music and Baby's Brain: Early Experience* 87.3 (2008) Web.

Brody, Gary. Interview. *Lovely Baby on the Radio*. WHPC-Nassau Community College, New York. 2012. Radio. <http://www.lovelybabycd.com/qa.html>.

Chamberlain, David. "Prenatal Stimulation: Experimental Results." *Birth Psychology*. The Association for Prenatal and Perinatal Psychology and Health, 2012. Web. 12 Dec. 2012. <http://birthpsychology.com/free-article/prenatal-stimulation-experimental-results>.

Heller, Linda. "Magic of Music." *Parents*. Aug. 1996: 120. Web.

Lecanuet, J.P., Graniere-Deferre, C., Jacquet, A. –Y., DeCasper, A.J. "Fetal Discrimination of Low- Pitched Musical Notes." John Wiley & Sons, Inc, 8 July 1999. Web. 8 Dec 2012. <http://www.ncbi.nlm.nih.gov/pubmed/10607359>.

Sorgen, Carol. "Bonding with Baby Before Birth." *WebMD*. WebMD, 2012
Web. 12 Dec. 2012.
<http://www.webmd.com/baby/features/bonding-with-baby-before-birth>.

Van de Carr, Rene. *While You Are Expecting: Create Your Own Prenatal
Classroom*. Humanics Pulishing Group, 1996. Print.

Warner, Peter. "The Mechanism of Mind-Manifesting Mushrooms."
Myko Web. 2004. Web. 7 Dec. 2012.
<http://www.mykoweb.com/articles/MindManifestingMushrooms.html>.

Zero to Three. National Center for Infants, Toddlers and Families, 2012. Web.
7 December 2012. <http://main.zerotothree.org/site/
PageServer?pagename=ter_key_brainFAQ#experience>.

NOT AS EASY AS IT ABEERS:

HOW TO POUR THE PERFECT PINT

IIIIIIIIIIIIIIIIIIIIIIIIIIIIIIIIIIIIIIIIIIIIIIIIIIIIIIIIIIIIIIIIIIIIIIIIIIIIIIIIII

Sam Crocker

When I applied for my first bartending job I thought serving drinks would be like working on a cash register at a grocery store, or being a waiter at a restaurant; I'd be repeating the same standard "Welcome to..." lines and doing the same boring jobs. Perhaps this was because I'd only just become old enough to even enter a bar or maybe I'd just never considered what the role involved, but by the end of my first week I had realized that I'd taken on a much more interesting and expansive position. The sacred role of bartender is bestowed upon those not only with the correct skills and commitment, but with an aptitude to learn fast on the job and to always be social with customers. You have to be quick thinking and always prepared to respond to new situations that might be thrust upon you during a busy night. If you want a job that tests your knowledge, social skills and speed of hand then bartending is the job to try. This article is aimed at providing a useful insight into bartending, as well as some essential tips for those looking to get started.

There are many skills you must learn to be a good barman: cocktail mixing, shot measuring, glass choices, customer relations, drink making routines… the list goes on. But without a doubt the most important skill any bartender must know is how to pour a beer correctly; if you can't pour the perfect beer, you can't really be considered a proper bartender. 'But that sounds simple?' you might be thinking. Wrong. Pouring beers from pumps can be a complicated skill to master. First time pourer Chris Shott commented "[…] my first pint was a frothy disaster. Its substantial head accounted for about two-thirds of the glass" ("Pour Self-Esteem"). Many people experience the same problems when starting. I would say it took me at least my first two months of pint pouring (this is probably well over a thousand beers) before I can truly say I 'mastered the pour'. Even now I still make the occasional mistake and might even have to start all over again. Here are my top tips for learning how to pour the perfect beer.

The Process

Greet the customer with a smile and take their order; unless specified as a half pint, the customer will usually mean a pint of beer if they say a particular brand. Grab the correct sized glass and place it underneath the corresponding tap at approximately a forty five degree angle. Pull the tap handle down towards you all the way, firmly and quickly. Let the beer flow down the side of the glass, this prevents the beer from aerating too much and creating head (froth on the top of the beer). Once the glass is around three quarters full, straighten it and fill all the way to the top before turning off the tap. The head on the top of any lagers, stouts or bitters you serve should be no larger than the width of your pinky finger but make sure there is a slight froth on the top of the pint, this keeps the beer fresh tasting and fizzy for longer. Interestingly British law even dictates that no more than 5% of the beer served is head ("More beer, less foam for Brits"). Make sure to serve the beer in front of the customer with your hand on the bottom half of the drink (this is marked by a groove on most common 'nonic' pint glasses) as the top section is for the customer's mouth only. Make sure to smile and say cheers!

Practice

As my Dad loves to tell me, "Practice makes permanent, not perfect!" Nobody pours their first beer correctly, most people don't pour their 50th perfect, but make sure that you always try to use the correct technique when pouring because if you practice incorrectly you will carry on pouring incorrectly too and eventually you will get caught, either by your manager, or more embarrassingly by your customer. Some poor pouring techniques I have seen in the past include: leaving the glass under the tap and walking away whilst it is pouring, holding the glass flat to create a massive head, dipping the nozzle of the tap inside the beer, or leaving no head so the beer looks more like urine than a drink.

Know your gear

Any barman will tell you the equipment in each bar varies in many different ways. In the bar I work in currently, there are approximately 30 different beer taps that I may need to use at any time and I know exactly how each one pours so I can get the perfect pint. Some will be frothy, some will be flat, some pour quickly, some can give out head if pushed in a certain way. To have a consistently good pint, you need to learn the personality of each pump. In many bars there are also special glasses for particular beers, so it is important to learn which glasses go with which beers.

Shandies and Dashes

Sometimes customers will ask for shandies, dashes or tops; this means that you need to also add lemonade to the glass to sweeten the beer. Make sure you put the lemonade in first or the beer will froth like mad. Shandies are half lemonade, half beer whilst dashes or tops are more like one fifth lemonade, four fifths beer. For thicker types of beer such as stouts, bitters and ales, the lemonade needs to be whisked to remove all bubbles before the beer is poured in.

Stouts, bitters, ciders and ales

Lagers are generally the most common beers that you will be pouring however, depending on what kind of bar you're working at, you may be asked to also pour different types of beers. As Sarah Pederson, the owner of Pasty Tavern in Oregon says "Depending on the type of beers you pour, you will need to pour them differently" ("How to Pour Tap Beer"). Just like you need to know the kit you work with, you'll be expected to know the characteristics of the different beers also. Stouts and bitters (e.g. Guinness, Newcastle Brown, and John Smiths) are poured three quarters full and left to rest for approximately one minute before the remainder of the glass is filled by pushing the tap away instead of pulling down. The company that produces Guinness, Diageo, advertises that "The perfect Guinness 'two-part pour' takes 119.5 seconds" ("Our Brands") but timing this maybe a little impractical so just make sure to finish your pour after the beer has stopped changing color (this is known as cascading). Ales usually come on traditional pulling lever pumps so simply place the glass under the spout and firmly but slowly pull the lever. Ales can be poured with a bubbly head or left slightly flat, and this can often depend on the type of ale. Ciders (for example Strongbow or Stowford Press) are poured strictly without a head and are often flat enough to be poured with the glass upright if you are feeling skillful.

So you're looking at getting into bartending? Don't know where to start? There are many different sorts of bars, each requiring different skill sets and attracting alternative clientele. This diagram should give you a brief idea of what kind of bars there are and which suit you best, so you know where to apply.

Type of drinking establishment	Speed of service	Type of service	Knowledge and skill level	Working hours
Old man pub	Rarely busy so speed is not needed	Have close relationship with customers	Serves similar drinks so skill needed is low	Can be day or night time
Cocktail bar	Urgency can be needed	Quality before quantity is important here	Reasonably high skill level to learn lots of drink recipes	Sometimes day but more often evenings
Club	Speed is of the essence!	An all-round good service combining speed and care	Have to make a wide range of drinks quickly and well	Usually night time until late
Expert	Speed not needed	Service of top quality	Highest level of knowledge and skill needed	Afternoons and evenings
Events	Varies depending on what type of event	Varies	Often low skill, good for beginners	Flexible and often single events

Each person will have their own personal preferences and skills for a particular style of bar work. It is important for you to find a style of bar that suits you best, you need to be enjoying your job for your customers to enjoy their experience at the bar. Don't be afraid to switch between bars if you think you are ready to take on a new challenge and never be afraid to ask a more experienced member of staff if you think you need help getting used to the position. You know you've found the right bar when it feels more like pleasure than work.

Who ever thought depositing liquid into a glass could be so complicated! The job of a bartender is a role that is greatly admired in social circles and can be a great way of building your customer relations skills. In New York State, you can start bartending from eighteen, so don't be afraid to go and try it for yourself! Follow these tips and you'll be making your own tips at the bar in no time!

Works Cited

Diageo. Advertisement. *Our Brands*. 2012. Web. *<.http://www.diageo.com/en-ie/ourbrands/categories/Pages/Beers.aspx>*.

Greble, Geoff. "A Master Brewer's Guide to Pouring the Perfect Guinness." Wegmans. 14 March 2012. Web. 2 October 2012. <http://www.wegmans.com/blog/2012/03/guide-to-pour-perfect-guinness/>.

Montgomery, Darrow. "Pour Self-Esteem". Washington City Paper. 11 May 2011. Image. Web. 8 October 2012. *<http://www.washingtoncitypaper.com/blogs/youngandhungry/2011/05/11/pour-self-esteem/>*.

"More beer, less foam for Brits." Deseret News. 19 March 2002. Web. 2 October 2012. *<http://www.deseretnews.com/article/902460/More-beer-less-foam-for-Brits.html?pg=all>*.

Pederson, Sarah. "How to Pour Tap Beer". eHow Food. Online presentation. *<http://www.ehow.com/video_6221872_pour-tap-beer.html>*.

Shott, Chris. "Pour Self-Esteem". Washington City Paper. 11 May 2011. Web. 8 October 2012. *<http://www.washingtoncitypaper.com/blogs/youngandhungry/2011/05/11/pour-self-esteem/>*.

HOLISTIC APPROACHES TO COMBATTING DEPRESSION

||||||||||||||||||||||||||||||||||||||||||||||||||||||||||||||||||||||||||||||

Kelli Lovdahl

Depression is an illness that affects millions of people worldwide, of all ages, backgrounds, income brackets, and life circumstances. I am a young woman who has firsthand seen loved ones suffer from this debilitating disease, and that has made me want to take a deeper look at the non-medicinal benefits that can be found through holistic healing approaches – focusing on mind-body awareness. Many people turn to psychotropic drugs and cognitive behavioral therapy to try to combat their depression symptoms, and many experience either no benefit or a relapse within just weeks or months of first seeing an improvement (La Torre 29). While for some individuals drugs may be enough to combat the issue, for many others it just doesn't cut it. By utilizing holistic approaches such as breathing techniques, meditation, herbal supplements, light therapy, and everyday lifestyle changes, people can begin to combat their depression from a much deeper source inside with successful and long-lasting results.

In Dr. Stephen Ilardi's book, The Depression Cure, he lays out a very simple 6-step method "to beat depression without drugs" (10). Ilardi describes combatting depression as an overall devotion to lifestyle change. He prefaces this statement by acknowledging that when one is depressed, motivation and goal-seeking actions are some of the first things to fail, which is why support is absolutely vital during the healing process (4). Ilardi says that lifestyle changes are necessary to combatting the disease of depression because our heavily modernized, chaotic lives have completely shifted away from our original role as human beings on this earth thousands of years ago, resulting in extreme imbalances in our bodies (6). He states that "the more modern a society's way of life, the higher its rate of depression…the human body was never designed for the modern post-industrial environment" (6). Because of these changes against the way we are "supposed" to be, Ilardi focuses on our most basic needs, drawn from a heavily evolutionary standpoint, that we lack a proper regulation because of modernization. His program involves the following lifestyle changes: vitamin and supplement intake, a complete reduction in ruminative thoughts, proper exercise, increased sunlight exposure either naturally or with a light box, social connection, and regular healthy sleep patterns (20).

There are a lot of holistic approaches to combatting depression that closely echo a similar mentality to Ilardi. These approaches tend to focus on combatting depression and anxiety through mindfulness, meditation, and guided relaxation. The concepts play off the idea of anti-ruminative thoughts, distracting one from whatever is worrying and clogging their mind and instead bringing the focus to a place that is "here and now". In this way, an individual grows more connected to their breath and their being, both bringing down the heart rate naturally and getting the mind off of racing, destructive thoughts and to a place that is calmer and peaceful (La Torre 28). Meditation is described as "a non-judgmental, present-moment experience that aids in focusing and has the advantage of self-management…it enhances relaxation, promotes self-esteem, and encourages behavioral change" (La Torre 29). Meditation has been proved to successfully reduce anxiety as much as medication such as Xanax and Ativan when practiced properly, while simultaneously empowering the person (La Torre 28). Anxiety is directly linked to depression, especially because of their common characteristic of worrying, ruminating thoughts – these thoughts can commonly spiral a person into a depressive episode. Learning how to gain awareness and insight into how to control the mind is vital when attempting to combat depression. With mindfulness and meditation, people learn about their physiological symptoms and how to train their bodies to react differently. With meditation, the heart rate can be trained to slow, breathing can become shallow and deeper, and racing thoughts can be calmed, to a level equaling those caused by medication (La Torre 30). Meditation can take away a lot of the agitating symptoms experienced by depressed and anxious individuals, without the risk of drug dependency.

After taking a look at holistic healing approaches, it seems that depression, while at times genetically caused, can also be a reflection of an unhealthy or imbalanced lifestyle. The fascinating research about the yogic chakras and different energy flows in the body show how a person can successfully create a happy and healthy life, when also dedicating oneself to lifestyle changes. Depression can cause other complications, like worrying, anxiety, fears, phobias, obsessive-compulsiveness, unexplained sickness and tiredness. The yogic mentality describes chakras as energy-filled areas of the body:

> While chakras are not considered to be physical, they frequently are associated with particular anatomical locations and are considered to have direct influenceo ver specific, select aspects of physical and mental functioning. (Maxwell 809)

This quote, taken from "The Neurobiology of Chakras and Prayer," describes the interesting phenomenon that an energy-filled place, though without a physical presence itself, can cause both mental and physical changes in the body. Through deeper research, it is evident that an imbalance in the chakra system can lead to depression. Similarly, if a depressed person works to strengthen these energy points, they can find extreme relief of their depressive symptoms (Kazak). There are seven main chakras in the body, located from the crown of the head to the pelvic area, radiating from the center-line of the body outward. Mary Horsley beautifully describes the curious nature of chakras in her book, *Chakra Workout*:

> The chakras can be likened to a series of doorways with keys to our development through life…the subtleties of the system are not that easy to communicate in words…true understanding of the chakras can be gained only through experience. (22)

Horsley's quote helps to describe the influential power of the chakras, although it is an idea that is difficult for one to wrap their mind around without trying it out. The idea of the chakras can seem a little "out there" or mystifying to people who are not totally sold on the idea of holistic healing, but there has been a strong, nearly 5,000 year history that tracks its benefits (Horsley 5). The seven main chakras are the following, with their Sanskrit counterparts listed in parenthesis: crown chakra (sahasrara, or thousand-petalled), third-eye chakra (ajna, or gateway of liberation), throat chakra (vishuddha, or purification), heart chakra (anahata, or the unstruck sound), solar plexus chakra (manipura, or gateway of the sun), sacral chakra (svadisthana, or home of the self), and root chakra (muladhara, or root support). Both the developmental and healing process of the seven chakras begins at the southernmost point of the root chakra, working steadily upward (Horsley 9).

Each of the chakras is responsible for their own set of outlooks, feelings, and experiences of life. If any of the chakras' energy is blocked, it can cause negative impacts throughout the body and mind (Kazak). For instance, the root chakra's purpose (located deep in the perineum of the human body) is devoted to the concepts of security and self-preservation, and when its energy is balanced it results in a person feeling secure, trusting, active and purposeful. When out of balance, it causes a person to feel insecurity, fear, distrust, indulgent, lethargic and possessive (Horsley 24). Within just one imbalanced chakra alone a person can feel depressive symptoms. When looking into how to strengthen the energy in the root, Horsley suggests that a person start to feel extremely grounded – getting in touch with nature, wearing red (the associated color of the root chakra), listening to tribal music with heavy drum beats, walk barefoot, eat organically to feel more connected to the earth, practice specific grounding yoga postures, and use meditation to visualize the body being deeply connected to the earth (28). If these routines are followed, the energy flows to the root get restored and result in a person letting go of the feelings of insecurity and fear, more able to control their impulsive self-indulgences and beginning the road to recovery (Horsley 31). Each of the remaining six chakras has its own set of values and characteristics, with its own means of strengthening the energy in order to build a strong, confident, grounded individual – from the inside outward.

Today, hospitals and medical facilities are slowly starting to introduce energy-healing practices as treatment programs, in the form of Reiki (Nemri 36). In this practice, a Reiki master puts their hands over the patient's body, over the different chakras or other energy points in the body where there is an ailment, either mental or physical. The Reiki master is a person that is deeply connected to spirituality, and therefore is believed to be able to align energy because of their keen awareness of a higher being. Much like the different chakra exercises can help to realign energy, the Reiki master is able to "force" energy into its proper state – in this way, it is very easy for the patient if they are having difficulties connecting to their own energy (Nemri 37).

Moderate depression is an illness that affects millions of people worldwide. Prescription drugs are written so frequently for this debilitating disease, but yet millions of people still remain depressed even after on medication (Cuijpers 1677). It has been proven that medication is minimally effective, or not effective at all, with people who have mild to moderate depression (however, for *severe* depression the success rates are higher). Oftentimes, people remain on these antidepressants for months, years or even for life – but can still suffer from their symptoms, having to additionally combat side effects as well as risk of drug dependency (Cuijpers 1684). Holistic approaches to combatting depression are the key ingredient to a person to become truly cured, from the very deepest inside parts out. Healing the chakras forces a person to really take a good, long look in the mirror and evaluate their characteristics, taking a hands-on approach to unblocking their energy that can be causing them so much physical and mental harm. While these holistic approaches prove to get a person into a more positive and "in-control" mindset, it also allows for spiritual growth and individual growth, as one learns about their strengths and weaknesses. The journey of healing depression can be thought of as a beautiful process, bringing light back into a person's life as they begin to truly understand their mind and their body – and *listen* to it. Holistic approaches, such as the 6-step program by Dr. Ilardi, meditation, mindfulness, Reiki, guided relaxation, and energy awareness through the chakras, can really change a person's life for the better – one hundred percent naturally.

Works Cited

Cuijpers, P. and A. Van Straten, et. al. "Are psychological and pharmacologic interventions equally effective in the treatment of adult depressive disorders? A meta-analysis of comparative studies." *Journal of Clinical Psychiatry* 69.11 (2008): 1675-1685. Web. 10 Nov 2012.

Horsley, Mary. *Chakra Workout: Balancing Your Energy with Yoga and Meditation.* New York, NY: Sterling Publishing Co., Inc., 2007. Print.

Ilardi, Stephen S. *The Depression Cure.* Cambridge, MA: Da Capo Press, 2009. Print.

Kazak, Sawsan. "Chakra Balancing." *Kuwait Times* 24 May 2012. Web. 28 Oct 2012.

La Torre, Mary Anne. "Integrative Perspectives: Therapeutic Approaches to Anxiety – A Holistic View." *Perspectives in Psychiatric Care* 37.1 (2001): 28-30. Print.

Maxwell, Richard W. and Ruth Stanley. "Neurobiology of Chakras and Prayer: *The Physiological Foundation of Yoga Chakra Expression.*" Zygon 44.4 (2009): 807-824. Print.

Nemri, Karin. "Aiigii Healing and How The Chakras Relate to Disease and Healing." *The Academy of Religion and Psychical Research Proceedings* (2004): 36-42. Print.

RENEWED, REFRESHED, & REVIVED

||||||||||||||||||||||||||||||||||||||||||||||||||||||||||||||||||||||||||||||||

Ciara Cristo

I've grown up with more than my fair share of support. When I wanted to play soccer, softball or tennis, my mother bought me every piece of equipment I could possibly require. It was clear after one softball game, in which I unintentionally gave a team member's brother a concussion, that I was not destined for athletic greatness. Once I found theater, I felt that I had found myself. However, given the very nature of theater and its multiple personalities, it became apparent that that was not an accurate assessment. From 2009 until recently, I grew increasingly more comfortable with labels, whether it be according to heritage or hobby. My crisis arose when I allowed myself to be typecast and stereotyped. I was now Ciara Cristo: *Thespian*. I was "that girl from the plays" and "the one who sings". I was voted *Best Actress* in my class and come graduation, was constantly approached with the phrases, "so you're studying theater, right?" and "remember me when you're on Broadway!". Ciara Cristo: *Thespian* was my evil Edward Hyde. As I fumble and fall through the coming years, and inevitably encounter new identity crises, I will myself to resist permanent transformation from Jekyll to Hyde.

Fear set in late in the game. I had just come off an incredible performance high. I had not frequently had the pleasure to play a leading role, but after finishing a run as the title role in a local production of *Peter Pan*, my confidence was sky high. That was until I entered the drafty audition room at Cohoes Music Hall. At fourteen-years-old with curves like Jessica Rabbit's, and a haircut reminiscent of John Lennon's circa 1965, my entire frame began to tremble. Before me sat the most sweet-tempered, friendly, men you ever did see. *What will you be singing for us?* The audio-visual delay I imagined between the movement of their lips and their voices startled me. All of a sudden, a million new fears hatched in my already reeling brain. I think I answered, but there's no way to know for sure. *Mama who bore me — mama who gave me no way to handle things; who made me so sad.* I continued singing my sixteen measures of the same song they'd been hearing for hours on end. The next sequence of events flew by me at lightning speed. I got a callback, was cast, and was given a solo in *Rent*. To this day, I contest that it was my unique, unflattering haircut that made me look like a 90's bohemian AIDS victim and merited my placement amongst the greatest young performers in the capital region. On January 9, 2009 at 8:00 pm, the butterflies returned. Opening night is always scary, but this one was in a whole other league. Song after song went by, and then it was my turn. My solo was 30 words: *How about a fur in perfect shape — owned by an MBA from uptown? I got a tweed broken in by agreedy broker who went broke, and then broke down.* Such an inconsequential moment in the show, but such a monumental one for a ninth grade girl with endless possibilities ahead of her. I stood tall downstage right with a pile of dirty old prop coats at my feet, and a sixteen-year-old drag queen in a Santa-baby dress to my left. The notes were simple, and the solo brief, but I felt like Ethel Merman and longed for a playbill to sign. When the adoring fans and movie deal didn't materialize before me, I didn't let it get me down, for this was where I was supposed to be. Instead, I snagged up every role I could within a fifty mile radius of my home with all the lingering conviction and optimism from the air I breathed in my fleeting moment of triumph.

The first thing I did after moving into my College of Charleston dorm in August, 2012 was go down to the campus bookstore and buy *Bossypants*. I held onto the book for dear life as I scurried back to my fifth floor suite dodging smokers and flying water balloons. Once in the safety of my room, I curled up with my coffee and let Tina reassure me, erasing all doubt and self-consciousness. In the span of four and a half years, I had changed my mind about my career path three million and five times. Whether it was arts management, international business, finance or film, I felt there was something standing in my way. Once Tina emphatically (and hilariously) explained the benefits of hard work and its tendency to yield to circumstance, my options became more promising. Though the economy hasn't mysteriously sprung back in accordance with her book sales, her words and conviction brought a sense of comfort and pragmatism to my befuddled brain. Now I can say with eighty-six percent confidence that I am a communications major? Okay, so I have some work to do on the career front, but at least I can rest easy knowing that someone as successful as she can also acknowledge that "perfect" is overrated. Of course I would die to write and act on *Saturday Night Live* or produce the next best NBC sitcom, but for now, I'm going to continue being contently confused and stressed. If life treats me half as well as it does Tina Fey, I'll gladly accept any debt, indecision, and uncertainty knowing that I'm not alone.

As you have now learned, I'm a bit of a theater geek. I'm not usually a fan of Rogers and Hammerstein, but they got a few things right with *The Sound of Music*. "Raindrops on roses and whiskers on kittens; bright copper kettles and warm woolen mittens; brown paper packages tied up with strings, these are a few of my favorite things". To anyone but Fraulein Maria, this list is meaningless, irrelevant and erratic. When the dog bites or bee stings, what will be there to pick you up? I have not been bestowed with Oscar Hammerstein's whimsical gift of rhyme, but I think my spirit-lifting list kicks ass.

› **Peanut Butter**—*America's Favorite Shmear*. I care not if it is Skippy, Jiff or Peter Pan and delivered by a serial killer to my front door—just let me be the first to scoop from it. The gratifying feeling of dipping a knife into a perfectly even surface of peanut butter falls just below college acceptance and just above winning a game of Monopoly.

› **Rear-View Mirror**—*The True Window Into the Soul*. Commuting to and from Saint Rose has put me on the road more often than not. As one who is not particularly fond of being behind the wheel, nothing brightens my early morning disposition like watching the rockstars behind me jam to the radio. Red lights are accepted—nay, encouraged—if it's a soccer-mom rapping.

› **Roasted Red Peppers**—*The Scent of the Heavens*. Generally speaking, people are opposed to stereotypes regarding their heritage or race. From my perspective, most Italian generalizations are pretty damn accurate. Many of my family members are hotheaded and traditional, but our most closely aligned stereotype is our passion for good food. While the Cristos have an undying love for pasta, bread and sauce, the smell of freshly roasted red peppers could pull me out of a coma.

› **Belting**—*A Soprano's Worst Nightmare*. Everyone deserves one sure-fire way to release pent up anger and aggression. Mine just happens to be singing Cole Porter's *"Anything Goes"* at the top of my lungs. Hitting that high C in my strongest belt is, and will always be, just what the doctor ordered. I love to read, and I'm a sucker for clever heist films, but when the dog bites, nothing hits the spot quite like a power-ballad.

Through all my phases, one thing has remained constant—they've each been documented, if only partially. Through thick and thin, I've been lucky to hold onto writing. Every so often I think I have experienced something worthy of an autobiography. I imagine who I would thank in my acknowledgements. *My mom for supporting me through it all; my dad for encouraging me to write. I thank Tina Fey for her inspiration and Cole Porter for composing the soundtrack of my life...* As I spend this time reflecting on the various editions of myself, it is clear that I've been brought back to basics. Each person has left his or her mark and I'm now faced with the daunting task of figuring out what's next. Perhaps an autobiography is in my future. Tina Fey will make a cameo appearance, as will Ciara Cristo: *Thespian*. Hopefully, years from now, their appearances will be greatly overshadowed by people and events that are yet to be. Until then, I'll bust my ass while waiting for destiny to crack me over the head with a cheap bottle of wine and a road map to success.

THE RISE OF iPADS IN THE CLASSROOM

||||||||||||||||||||||||||||||||||||||||||||||||||||||||||||||||||||||||||||||||

Sarah Watson

Imagine sitting in a classroom and having the opportunity to use an iPad to assist you in your education. Well, today in many Elementary Special Education classrooms, the iPad is the newest piece of assistive technology that is being used. Assistive Technology is "any item, piece of equipment, or product system, whether acquired commercially off the shelf, modified or customized, that is used to increase, maintain or improve functional capabilities of individuals with disabilities" (Cavanaugh 1). Assistive technology has many benefits for students with disabilities. Terence Cavanaugh states in *Assistive Technology and Inclusion* that it has "the capacity for increasing student independence, increasing participation in classroom activities and simultaneously advancing academic standing for students with special needs" (4). Students are able to participate in classroom discussion with the service of assistive technology and also their academic progress rises because of the assistive technology.

Assistive technology has evolved from computers and Dynavox's to iPads and other tablets to assist students with disabilities improve in literacy and other subjects. The iPad is being used in special education classrooms all over the country to help disabled students find their voice by allowing them to participate in classroom discussions. There are a variety of applications that can be used on the iPad that help students with disabilities work in classrooms with their peers as well as communicate outside of the classroom. The iPad is the most recent advancement in assistive technology in Special Education classrooms and with it's simple interface, portability, affordability and abundance of applications, it gives students with disabilities an easier opportunity to reach their literacy goals.

Assistive technology in special education classrooms has developed rapidly over the years. Nirvi Shah states in an Education Week article, the iPad has replaced "bulky, expensive older forms of assistive technology" (16). An example of this type of bulky, expensive type of assistive technology is speech generating devices such as DynaVoxMaestro and DynaVoxDynaWrite2.0. DynaVox is a company that was built in 1983 and manufactures and distributes speech generating devices. The speech generating devices known as Dynavox assists special education students in communication and provides assistance for educational purposes (DynaVoxtech.com). The DynaVox has been helping thousands of people whose speech is restricted. (DynaVoxtech.com) Although the DynaVox is still a beneficial tool for many individuals with disabilities; Dynavox's are being placed on the backburner due to high cost and unreliability. A Dynavox can cost up to $8,000 and can be a sticky situation when dealing with insurance coverage. Many special educators are now selecting assistive technology that is both more useful and less expensive.

Desktop computers and laptops are also becoming a technology of the past. The usage of laptops by students has been experimented in the past but wheeling the laptop cart from classroom to classroom posed a hassle for many students and educators. Some of the laptops would not be charged, some would have keys missing and no one was taking responsibility for them (Shah 17). Dynavox's and computers are still used in classrooms however, as technology is rapidly developing, these types of assistive technology are being replaced by the iPad.

A tool that paves a fresh path of learning is the iPad (Shah 16). "The iPad offers a sense of independence with many children, especially those with disabilities…" (Shah 16). The iPad's "simple interface, portability, speed and affordability, combined with highly engaging nature of many of their applications ("apps"), present intriguing alternatives to expensive high-tech tools" (Dell and Newton 55). These aspects add an ease in using an iPad which is beneficial for many students and educators. IPad's can be used for any subject in the classroom however; communication and literacy are popular uses of the iPad especially for students who are Autistic and struggle with communication and language. Not only does the iPad help in school but also helps with life skills such as ordering at a restaurant or purchasing items at the grocery store (Shah 17). The iPad has all the modalities, sound and touch that is best suited for students with disabilities, with the advancement in technology, traditional media cannot compete with this product (Shah 16). The interface of an iPad is an important aspect of assistive technology and Shah states this by saying that the "touch screen design is easier to use than a desktop computer with a mouse or laptop with a touchpad" (16). The 4G iPad starts at $499 and can increase from there depending on what features and applications are purchased on the iPad. Many students with disabilities can get hung up on the challenges of technology because of their lack in focus; however the iPad is less of a challenge for students because it offers a sense of "instant gratification for students with limited patience" (Shah 17) so the students will be able to focus on their work rather than wasting time figuring out the technology.

The iPad offers many possibilities for students with disabilities so I took the opportunity to go to New Scotland Elementary School in Albany, NY, in hopes of talking with two teachers about the usage of technology in their special education classrooms.

I met with Mrs. Harris who works in a Co-Teacher third grade classroom. A Co-Teacher classroom consists of a regular education teacher, a special education teacher and a teacher's assistant. This classroom has ten identified special education students. While talking to Mrs. Harris, I discovered that technology does not play a big role in her classroom. Although this classroom does not focus heavily on using the iPad or Dynavox, I found out that two students use a type of assistive technology to help with their focus in the classroom. One student uses a sensory pad that he sits on to comfort his sensory issues. He also has a black piece of paper that stays on his desk that helps him to focus on his work. I also found out that a girl rips pieces of sticky-note paper to comfort her with her sensory issues as well. Although the sensory cushion, black piece of paper and sticky notes are not considered "typical" assistive technology such as an iPad or Dynavox, they are still considered assistive technology because they are "used to increase, maintain, or improve functional capabilities of individuals with disabilities" (Cavanaugh 1). These items used do benefit the students in this classroom, and therefore are considered assistive technology.

Next, I met with Ms. Ocel who is the speech teacher at New Scotland Elementary School and works in a self-contained classroom grades K-5. I was hoping to learn about the iPad and how they used in them in the classroom. Ms. Ocel mentioned that in the self-contained classrooms this year there are no students that are completely non-verbal so the students do not use DynaVox. Rather than using the Dynavox, the types of assistive technology that are used in the classroom are SmartBoards, touch screens on the computers and the iPad. Ms. Ocel claims that the iPad "is the best speech tool that I have ever had if I could have used it earlier I would have. It incorporates speech, reading, writing, math everything." The iPad is a very effective type of assistive technology especially because many of the students in the self-contained classroom are visual learners and using the interactive touch screen assists their visual needs. Ms. Ocel feels that the students are making the most progress since purchasing the iPads last year. Ms. Ocel also mentioned that the iPad is able to receive the most updated programs. Having the most up to date programs is most beneficial for students with disabilities. Working with the iPad can be more effective for students with disabilities because many students cannot write on paper and some students struggle to get their ideas out on pen and paper. In the literacy aspect of a student's education, Ms. Ocel mentioned different applications (apps) on the iPad that the students are able to use such as Tap to Talk which is voice output/ vocabulary, PocketPhonics which works on beginning sounds, and house for learning which works on prepositions, vocabulary, following directions, and storytelling. I was able to get a document that had all the applications they use in the classroom which consists of about thirty applications the classrooms uses. Also, I received a link to check out more applications that can be used. The iPads are also beneficial for the students to communicate with their peers.

Learning how beneficial and useful the iPad is in the classroom, I wanted to research what applications are used. The interface of an iPad "offers content-specific information in a convenient and captivating format" (Dell and Newton 55), which makes it easier for students to work with and easier for educators to program for each individual student. The importance of technology in the classroom is rapidly increasing however; the technology that is used by each student should be programmed for their needs. Cavanaugh talks of how some assistive devices are shared among a group of individuals therefore they are not programmed for one individual's needs (4). The applications create the ability for students with disabilities to focus on one portion at a time rather than getting distracted especially for students who have visual perceptual difficulties, reading disabilities and/or attention issues (Dell and Newton 55). There are hundreds of applications also known as apps that are free, have a cost or are included in the software on the iPad.

The iPad is a model for an eBook just like a kindle. An eBook "was designed for viewing digital text on a portable, book-like device" (Bayliss, Connell and Farmer 132). A popular reading application is *iBook*. Using the *iBook* application on the iPad is beneficial because of the iPad's "high-resolution LCD display" (Bayliss, Connell and Farmer 132). The *iBook* application makes the iPad an eBook. A study has been done about the effectiveness of the eBook style of reading in special education classrooms and it is claimed that readers are able to perceive particular types of screen text due to the bigger screen (Bayliss, Connell and Farmer 133) Also, "reading comprehension was better for those who flipped their virtual pages" (Bayliss, Connell and Farmer 133). When a student with a disability is able to interact with the reading, they are better able to comprehend; therefore this application benefits their literacy learning. A study was also done on strategies that were used to improve comprehension skills of students, the *Journal of Special Education Technology* claimed that teachers "revealed that students benefited from listening to a story multiple times" (Douglas, Ayres, Langone, Bell and Meade 38). Students with disabilities who work with the *iBook* app allows students to read a text over and over and by seeing it highlighted creates a connection between understanding what they see on the interface and understand what they are reading.

When using the *iBook* application, students can read different types of material such as books or PDF files while having access to a "dictionary, thesaurus, font size and style changer, search feature, bookmarks, highlighting and sticky note inserts" (Dell and Newton 56). When text is being highlighted and read aloud for students with disabilities, it can improve their comprehension and unaided reading (Douglas, Ayres, Langone, Bell and Meade 37). This gives students the opportunity to read on a different device while still being able to do all the things they could do in a paperback book.

Reading comprehension and literacy go hand in hand in a special education classroom and researching about applications, there are an abundance of applications. An application called *The Cat in the Hat* allows students to either get read to, read it to themselves or auto play. Also, they can listen to the story by the narrator while the words get highlighted, read it like a traditional book or watch it like a movie (Dell and Newton 56).

While there are many applications for reading, there are many applications for writing. An application used for learning the alphabet and working on hand writing skills is *iWriteWords*. This application lets students use their finger to draw letters, practice handwriting and letter recognition (Dell and Newton 56). Applications that assist with word processing and handwriting are *Speak it! Text to Speech, Typ-O HD and WritePad* (Dell and Newton 57). Two applications that can assist with note taking are AudioNote-Notepad and Voice Recorder which can record their "teachers lectures while writing or typing only key words" (Dell and Newton 57). Many students with disabilities struggle with organization. There are four applications that can help dealing with organization. One application is *iCal* which is a calendar application. Also, iHomework which sets a study reminder, tracks assignments and grades and paces long term projects, Todo which is a to-do list and project manager and *iThoughts* which can be used for brainstorming, project planning and concept mapping (Dell and Newton 57). There are also plenty of applications for students with severe disabilities that assist in communication of the students and communication with the parents or guardians.

Assistive Technology has progressed rapidly over the years and will continue to progress. As I am planning to become an elementary special education teacher, learning about the iPad and keeping up with the advances means using the most effective and beneficial technology for my students. Being able to program a student's technology to fit their learning style only increases their chances for achieving their biggest goals which will be my job as an educator. Applications on the iPad are developing and are able to assist in any subject in school but also in everyday skills. The change in assistive technology in classrooms means a change in the ways that students learn and the types of skills the students learn.

Works Cited

Bayliss Lauren, Connell, Caroline, Farmer, Whitney "Effects of eBook Readers and Tablet Computers on Reading Comprehension." *International Journal of Instructional Media* (2012): 131-40. Print.

Cavanaugh, Terence W. "Assistive Technology and Inclusion." *ATEN-Assistive Technology Education Network.* (2002): 1-7. Print.

Dell Amy G., Newton Deborah A. "Assistive Technology." *Journal of Special Education Technology* (2011): 59-60. Print.

Douglas, Karen H., Ayres, Kevin M., Langone, John, Bell, Virginia and Meade, Cara "Expanding Literacy for Learners with Intellectual Disabilites: The Role of Supported eText." *Journal of Special Education Technology* (2009): 35-44. Print.

Shah, Nirvi. "Special Ed. Pupils Find Learning Tool in iPad Applications." *Editorial Projects in Education* 30.22 (2011): 15-7. Print.

Speech Devices - Augmentative Communication | DynaVox." *Communication Devices â" Speech Devices | DynaVox.* N.p., n.d. Web. 18 Nov. 2012. <http://www.dynavoxtech.com/default.aspx>

NOTES ON 'DUDE'

||||||||||||||||||||||||||||||||||||||||||||||||||||||||||||||||||||||||||||||

Rachel Gagnon

1. Dude is slang for:

   a. A man excessively concerned with his clothes, grooming, and manners.

   b. A fellow; chap.

   c. A general term of address used to a man, woman, or group).

   d. A person reared in a large city.

   e. An urban Easterner who vacations on a ranch.

It is also important to note that Dude can also be used as an exclamation, with a wide variety of meanings based on the tone, pitch, cadence, and facial expression used by the speaker.

2. The Dude attitude is one of a lackadaisical, irresponsible, passive individual when used in the context of an individual in the 1970s; namely the surfer. However, when looking at Dude in terms of its older definition, it is derived from the well dressed, overly meticulous when it comes to apparel, manners,

and grooming, especially for wealthy property owners or city slickers that owned land in the Mid-West.

3. Dude is not only a way of identifying a specific person or group, but also there are characteristics, or characters rather, that have the "Dude" mentality. These characters are more prevalent in 1980s and 1990s teen comedy movies, but also appear in more sophisticated cinema. The Dude lifestyle can be seen as a laid-back lifestyle, with a hint of slacker spice.

4. Some examples defining, pontificating, and emulating Dude, in no particular order:

Joel and Ethan Coen's The Big Lebowski

Surfing

Cheese in a can

Skateboarding

Males with long hair

Males with long hair who consistently touch their hair with the occasional head shake to fix their hair

The State of California

Marijuana

Snowboarding

Boarding school dropouts

Teenage boys

Teenage male athletes after consuming alcohol

A girl that is close friends with a boy, i.e.-'one of the boys'

Doritos

Woven hemp wristbands

Lava lamps

Tie dye

Oversize flannel shirts

No shirt

Beanbag chairs

Drool

Anything described as 'gnarly'

Beaches

Chamomile tea

Open-toed Jesus sandals

No shoes

The electric guitar

Air guitar

Dude, Where's My Car?

Cowboy boots

Cattle ranches

Chicken bacon ranch pizza

Expensive pants

No pants

5. A Dude can have a taste in art, but the 'taste' being referred to is altogether a delusion on the Dude's part. In other words, most Dudes do not have any prior knowledge of art.

6. Art is selected based on either visual distraction (stimulation) or reputation.

7. An example would be to select a 'trippy' tie-dye illustration or painting, because of its colorful, distracting quality.

8. Another example would be for a Dude to select an artwork that is made by a world-renown artist such as Pablo Picasso, Salvador Dali, or Vincent Van Gogh. This artists particularly because of their unique and again, 'trippy' styles of painting.

9. Still nothing is known about the work, only that it is said to be great, therefore making the Dude's taste in art spectacular.

10. It does not matter if it is a strong piece of art, or cliché pieces of rubbish; if a Dude is distracted, then they are convinced.

11. It is merely by means of strengthening their egos that Dudes purchase art, if at all.

12. Some might say, "If you're a Dude, you're Dumb."

13. When referring to a Dude or speaking in a Dude manner, one assumes the Dude affiliate to be less intelligent than the average person. To be Dude is to not be the sharpest tack in the box, the brightest bulb in the lamp, or the quickest fish in the brook.

14. All Dude paraphernalia, phrases, and ways of life at least somewhat immature. A youthful essence, if you will. Even old Dudes classify due to the lack of mature list of priorities and accomplishments. Dudes are either not yet grown up, meaning they are still teenagers or young adults, or they never will grow up, and their minds stay childish.

15. Dude is to push away worries such as education, benefiting society, money, and the expiration date on milk. In return for this lifestyle, Dudes do not reap the benefits of a quality education, and speak slower, think slower, and feel most at ease when chill.

16. When Dudes speak, it is in order to draw out a word for emphasis. It is not a sweet car, it is a sweeeet carrrr.

17. The history of dude is an uncertain one, though there are many theories. One such theory is that the word is derived from the word 'dud', as in, "My, that cowboy has a sweet pair of duds. I wish I dressed that well!" when referring to nice clothing. The term was then later used in the 1920s to describe a dude ranch, which is a cattle ranch where rich men would vacation and pretend to be rough n' tough cowpokes living on nothing but beef jerky and their own sweat, never tears. In reality however, these wealthy men never wanted to get dirty or ruin their clothing, hence their 'duds' on a 'dude' ranch. Somehow, the general surfing population decided to add the word to their expansive vocabulary, and thus Dude was born. Dude is then later used by a plethora of adolescent youth; namely male, sometimes smoking reefer, almost always awkward with ladies.

18. There is an almost innocent aspect to Dude, mainly because of its childish and immature nature. If a Dude were to be for the sake of discussion, under the influence of LSD, and having a bad experience, one would either laugh or try to comfort the shaking and scared Dude. Depending on the personality of the observer, of course.

19. There are several ways that Dude can be interpreted when used as an exclamation: in awe, surprise, appreciation, anger, sadness, disgust, disappointment, shock, disapproval, sympathy, excitement, reproving, etc.

20. Here are some examples I have created for further understanding:

21. Reproving: "Hey man, I hope you don't mind that I got tapioca on your brand-new bowling shirt." "Dude..."

22. Excitement: "Dude! I just won a new pair of scissors on the radio! Sick!"

23. Anger: "Dude! What the eff, man? That's my mom!"

24. Sympathy: "Yo, you are not going to believe this bro, but I lost my front-row seat ticket for Creedence tomorrow." "Dude. Bummer."

25. Awe: "Dude. That chick has got the wine in the bottle, if you know what I mean."

26. Disgust: "And then he had the nerve to use that cheesy wine bottle pick-up line on me!" "Dude, that's ridiculous!"

27. Shock: "Dude! No way! I bought a new VCR too!"

28. Appreciation: "You traded your car for a brand-new bong? Dude...You are a lucky man.

29. Males are not the only ones who use the term Dude. Although not as conventional, female use of the term Dude is on the rise.

30. According to a survey done by noted dudeologist Scott F. Kiesling, females use Dude twice as much towards other females than they do towards males (283).

31. Other variations of Dude have surfaced since the word was first used. Among them are bro, chum, son, bud, buddy, man, kid, etc.

32. To be a Dude, one must not be afraid to sound stupid.

33. The hallmark of Dude is to not care about anything except for what you are eating, and if you are cold, warm, or sleepy.

34. What is not Dude, but is rather close are those that are referred to as hippies.

35. Hippies are not Dude because of the element of love.

36. Dude does not love. Dude just chills.

37. To chill is to just be with the present moment and not judge it or fight it, but accept it.

38. There are two types of Dudes: active and inactive.

39. The active Dude skates, surfs, or snowboards. The inactive Dude surfs the TV. MTV is usually the channel of choice, namely for the music videos.

40. Cheese products are for the most part a very important aspect of Dude living. Perhaps it is because cheesy foods are commonly used to reference foods associated with the munchies.

41. The munchies is a period of time which occurs after a person is under the influence of cannabis, wherein the consumer will have the ability and desire to eat large quantities of food that he otherwise would not be able to keep down.

42. Dudes are often associated with pot, causing them not to function in a completely focused, alert, or active way.

43. Dude is a middle finger so to speak, to the capitalist, money grabbing and fast-paced society that we live in today. "The Dude abides"- Jeffrey Bridges as his character 'The Dude' in The Big Lebowski

44. In the Coen Brothers movie The Big Lebowski, the 'hero' is a man known simply as 'The Dude.'

45. No other movie has exploited the stereotypical image of Dude as much as The Big Lebowski.

46. The Dude's clothes are a bathrobe, boxers, a t shirt, a sweater, and the occasional bowling shirt and sunglasses.

47. The Dude's manner of speech is limited, although he can be surprisingly verbose at times.

48. The Dude's lifestyle- sleeping, baths with candles, listening to music, and bowling

49. The Dude's diet i.e. - joints, beer, coffee, and White Russian (a cocktail of vodka, cream, and Kahlúa)

50. In The Big Lebowski, the Dude is tossed about in a never-ending situational cyclone, devoid of any control. All that The Dude wants in life is to smoke his marijuana, drink his White Russian, listen to Creedence, and spend time with his friends bowling. He is happy to live life simply and without anger, grudges, confrontations, or mishaps.

51. No matter what ridiculous situation The Dude is put into, or how many people are chasing him for his life, The Dude abides, and carries on to seek his simple pleasures.

52. Despite the ignorant or unintelligent appearance and manner of The Dude, the character is really quite complex and can be interpreted in different ways.

53. Thus The Dude can be interpreted as having a likeness to a Zen or Buddha figure, so to speak; what matters most to the Dude in life stays consistent regardless of the negative happenings which are out of his control. He creates his own happiness, and is accepting and comfortable with who he is as an individual.

54. Another interpretation of The Dude is that of a schlemiel figure. Schlemiel is a Yiddish word meaning, "an awkward and unlucky person for whom things never turn out right."

55. As previously mentioned in Note no. 44, The Dude is reserved in that he does not control his surroundings, and would rather stay at home and be comfortable than be out stirring trouble or causing problems. In "The Dude As Modern Hero? Salvation And Jewish Storytelling In The Big Lebowski," Eitan Kensky writes about this submissiveness. He writes, "It is partly this passivity that characterizes the Dude as schlemiel" (8). This seems to be a fairly accurate perception, seeing as The Dude is a likable character who is always getting shoved, pushed, hit, and toilet head-dunked, without any way to halt the attacks that life seems to be throwing at him.

56. However, Kensky also writes that this "schlemiel role…is only a part of his character and not the essential element" (9). This may not be completely correct, for without The Dude completely drenched in the role of the schlemiel, the entire film would lack structure and cohesion. There would be no way to transition between plotlines; no means of unity that helps the viewer understand the relationships between subjects and characters.

57. In the end, The Dude brings a different background and history to the meaning of 'Dude', one deriving from Jewish storytelling, and influences the way Dude is used and thought of henceforth.

58. The term Dude has affected society and adolescents in a way that has made the English language more personal, more accessible, and more sweet, dude.

Works Cited

Ashe, Fred. "The Really Big Sleep: Jeffrey Lebowski as the Second Coming of Rip Van Winkle." *The Year's Work in Lebowski Studies*. 41-57. Bloomington, IN: Indiana UP, 2009. MLA International Bibliography. Web. 26 Oct. 2012.

The Big Lebowski. Dir. Joel Coen. Perf. Jeff Bridges, John Goodman, and Julianne Moore. Working Title Films, 1998. DVD.

"dude." *Collins English Dictionary - Complete & Unabridged 10th Edition*. HarperCollins Publishers. Web. 12 Oct. 2012

"dude." *Dictionary of Contemporary Slang*. London: A&C Black, 2007. Credo Reference. Web. 12 October 2012.

"duds." *Dictionary of Contemporary Slang*. London: A&C Black, 2007. Credo Reference. Web. 12 October 2012.

Hill, Richard A. "You've Come a Long Way, Dude: A History." *American Speech*. 69.3 (1994): 321-327. JSTOR *Arts & Sciences III*. Web. 26 Oct. 2012.

Kensky, Eitan. "The Dude as Modern Hero? Salvation and Jewish Storytelling in The Big Lebowski." *Americana: The Journal Of American Popular Culture (1900-Present)*. 9.1 (2010): MLA International Bibliography. Web. 12 Oct. 2012.

Kiesling, Scott F. "Dude." *American Speech*. 79.3 (2004): 281-305. Communication & Mass Media Complete. Web. 12 Oct. 2012.

"schlemiel." *Collins English Dictionary - Complete & Unabridged 10th Edition*. HarperCollins Publishers. Web. 19 Oct. 2012.

"white russian." *Collins English Dictionary - Complete & Unabridged 10th Edition*. HarperCollins Publishers. Web. 19 Oct. 2012.